Who *Really* Saved

Savannah?

The Surprising Paradox

Jack C. Wray

 www.trafford.com

North America & international
toll-free: 1 888 232 4444 (USA & Canada)
fax: 812 355 4082

Contents

—⌒ *Preface* ⌒—

When I moved to Savannah thirty-five years ago, I had no idea how much God's providential grace would change my life. All through my high school, college, and seminary education, I did everything I could to run away from history courses. I hated history! But ten years ago, when Karen and I joined St. John's Episcopal Church, my life began to change drastically. St. John's owns the beautiful, historic Green-Meldrim House standing next to the church. The Green-Meldrim tour-guide chairman, Jane Pressly, asked me if I would be interested in being a docent for the beautiful house tours. I reluctantly agreed and immediately found myself immersed in a treasure of history that completely captured my interest and inspired my passion for a severely neglected part of my life. Realizing what a gold mine of history Savannah is, I soon got licensed with the city to do walking tours, spent two years driving and narrating carriage tours, and now am consumed with research for my walking-tour business with a passionate emphasis on accuracy.

My love of history in Savannah has narrowed to researching the experience of what it meant for the beautiful city and its leaders to survive the horrific fifty-three days of Sherman's occupation of Savannah and his stay with Charles Green. I also immediately discovered that much of the War history of Sherman, Jefferson Davis, Robert E. Lee, Abraham Lincoln, Ulysses Grant, and others has been shaped by mythical folklore passed down as accurate history through our education system and Hollywood movie writers and directors. The Southern Cause has been scrubbed! And what better place to pull the curtain back and view the history of the Southern Cause than here in Savannah. I have a burning passion for introducing tourists to historical accuracy. After all, tourism is the second major income driver of the Savannah economy.

Savannah is one of the ten most-sought travel destinations here and abroad. Her Southern charm, her well--preserved nineteenth-century architecture, her beautiful squares and brilliant city plan, her mystique, her attraction for Hollywood filming sites, and her casual—yes, slow—pace bring millions of tourists to visit every year. In 2013, thirteen million tourists spent over $2 billion in Savannah. Tourism grows in leaps every year.

SAVANNAH 2015

Image P-a

But it hasn't always been that way for the Southern Lady. She has faced many close calls with destruction, including fires, plagues, wars, and a market crash in 1892, which was worse than the one in 1928. Yet through each impending disaster, her survival can be attributed solely to providential grace.

One of the closest calls to total disaster happened in December of 1864 with the arrival of sixty-two thousand Union troops and Gen. William T. Sherman, or Uncle Billy, as his boys called him. This fifty-three-day heart-pounding, nail-biting, hair-raising horror story of her onion-skin-thin bare survival centers on the central question: **who saved Savannah—*really?***

Image P-b

For fifty-three days, key players in their own way took steps toward Savannah's survival very much like a string of dominos, lined up perfectly, falling in her favor—providentially. So who was the one ultimately responsible for saving Savannah from disaster? Was it Sherman or Confederate general William Hardee? Was it Abraham Lincoln or Dr. Richard Arnold, the mayor in 1864? How about secretary of war Edwin Stanton or Savannah's beloved Charles Green? Was it Union general John Geary or some insignificant other? Among all the key players on both the Northern and the Southern side of the War, one, in particular, made the singular call that saved our beautiful city. His name will surface later in a surprising paradox.

In the following chapters, we will explore in detail just how Savannah survived: (1) Sherman's Georgia campaign, (2) arrival outside Savannah: Hardee's daunting gray stop sign, (3) capture of Fort McAllister, (4) Sherman in Carolina with Gen. John Foster, (5) Hardee's brazen bluff, (6) evacuation of Confederate troops, (7) Mayor Arnold's meeting and letter, (8) Mayor Arnold and Gen. John Geary, (9) Charles Green's brilliant business decision, and (10) Sherman in Savannah.

Throughout the book, I will use the word 'War' to refer to what most people call the civil war. This is my Southern bias bleeding through because there was nothing civil about this War, as you will see in chapter 1. Other names often used are the War between the States, the War of Northern Aggression, the War of Southern Secession, or the War of Southern Independence. However, my favorite name comes from Professor Edward C. Smith in his presentation, "Mixed Up With All The Rebel Horde," to the Sons of Confederate Veterans national convention on August 12, 1993, in Lexington, Kentucky. He calls it 'The Second Revolution.'

Gene Kizer Jr., in his recent (2014) book, *Slavery Was Not the Cause of the War Between the States,* chapter 5, "The Right of Secession," expounds a thoroughly detailed comparison of the Revolutionary War and the War of Southern Secession. This chapter details how the Constitution of the United States, framed by our Founding Fathers, set the basis for the right of any state to secede from the Union without fear of reprisal. Thomas Jefferson included in the Constitution the critical principle that governments

> ***derive their just powers from the consent of the governed; and that, whenever any form of government becomes destructive of these ends, it is the right of the people to alter or abolish it, and to institute a new government.***

The conclusion of this thoroughly outlined chapter positions the Revolutionary War, 1775–1783, identically parallel to the War of Southern Secession seventy-six years later, 1861–1865, and, thus, can be correctly called The Second Revolutionary War.[1]

This book is an absolute must for any serious student of nineteenth-century history.

---

[1] . Gene Kizer Jr., *Slavery Was Not the Cause of the War between the States,* 2014, pgs. 70–75.

Acknowledgments

I owe much gratitude to several important people who convinced me and supported me in taking on this project. First, to the Green-Meldrim House tour-guide chairman, Jane Pressly. If it weren't for her, I would probably still hate history and keep running away from it. But her smiling personality and gentle invitation, as anyone who knows her will attest, is impossible to resist.

Second, my dear friend and companion on trips all over Georgia visiting SCV camps and historical places, Donald A. Newman. Don is the commander of the Savannah Militia, Camp 1657, Sons of Confederate Veterans - the Georgia Division's largest camp (152 members) and continually increasing. Don is a walking encyclopedia of War history, not only in Savannah but all throughout the United States. The speakers he invites for monthly programs and the occasional programs he often presents himself are loaded with historical stories not found in history books. Having never heard it presented the way I did on PowerPoint for one of our camp programs, he continued to encourage me to write the narrative of Savannah's survival.

Third, the many people who watched the Power Point presentation of Savannah's survival and strongly encouraged me to have the narrative published. So many folks, including veteran tour guides, said it needed to be published and convinced me to undertake writing a narrative of the presentation.

Fourth, my wife, Karen, who continually kept me focused on task to write this book and encouraged me to stay with it. She is a very task-oriented, structured person, who would not let me off the hook. Many thanks to her.

And last, this book is dedicated to my son, J. Derek Wray, who stands in line to carry the baton of honoring our ancestor, Thomas G. Elmore. He enlisted on September 1, 1862, at Wake County, North Carolina, as a private in Company H of the Forty-Fifth North Carolina Infantry, was wounded and hospitalized on June 4, 1864, in Danville, Virginia, returned to active duty June 15, 1864, was a prisoner of war on March 25, 1865, in Petersburg, Virginia, and confined March 28, 1865, at Point Lookout, Maryland. He is my son's great-great grandfather who survived the War, moved back home to Midway, North Carolina, died in 1905, and is buried at Midway United Methodist Church.

⁓ᴄ͡ɔ One ᴄ͡ɔ⁓

Sherman's Georgia Campaign

In early May 1864, Union general William T. Sherman and sixty-two thousand troops began the Atlanta Campaign to take the city. By early July, the Confederate forces were backed up against the outskirts of Atlanta. With Confederate supply lines fully severed, Confederate general John Bell Hood pulled his troops out of Atlanta on September 1, destroying supply depots as he left to prevent them from falling into Union hands. He also set fire to eighty-one loaded ammunition cars, which led to a huge destructive fire watched by hundreds.

The next day, September 2, Mayor James Calhoun met a captain on the staff of Union general Henry W. Slocum and surrendered the city, asking for "protection to noncombatants and private property." Sherman sent a telegram to Lincoln on September 3, which reads, "Atlanta is ours, and fairly won." He then established his headquarters there on September 7 and stayed for over two months.

Burning of Atlanta

Image 1-a

On November 15, Sherman left the remainder of Atlanta in smoke and ashes, burning everything left for Confederates to salvage, and set out on his Georgia campaign in what was called his infamous March to the Sea.

It is important to pause before proceeding to look at that title, March to the Sea. Those were not just four nebulously chosen words randomly pulled out of the sky, forming a nice-sounding phrase. No! Those four words were very carefully chosen with a purpose.

To get at their importance, it is necessary to go back through your knowledge of American history and rewind to pre-Sherman Atlanta, say, around early spring 1864. Then you have to delete from your brain everything you know about Southern history, the way you hit the Delete key on your computer. You are now at the time when Sherman has not yet arrived in Atlanta. The city is calm for the moment.

Now picture yourself talking to your next-door neighbor along these lines: "Wouldn't it be nice to take a trip this summer and go to the beach or the sea or the ocean and have a nice, leisure vacation walking the beach?" And you continue dreaming with your neighbor for a while. Now just thinking about such a hypothetical conversation, answer this question. Relative to Atlanta way up in the northwest corner of the face of Georgia, where is the sea? Back then, you would realize the sea is the whole eastern sea coast, all the way from Nova Scotia to Key West, Florida. Now relative to Atlanta, the sea with respect to Georgia is Savannah, Richmond Hill, Darien, Brunswick, and Kingsland, all the way to St. Marys on the Florida line—one hundred miles of Georgia coast.

Now what have you done? You have discovered that the four words "March to the Sea" do not disclose a destination. Those words are a military strategy! Only five people knew the destination:

Lincoln, who signed off on the atrocities about to happen; secretary of war Edwin Stanton, who also signed off on the atrocities about to happen; Union general Ulysses Grant, who signed off on the atrocities and encouraged Sherman to proceed with his plan in spite of his caution; and two Union generals heading the sixty-two thousand Union soldiers—Gen. Otis Oliver Howard and Major Gen. Henry Slocum. Even the sixty-two thousand soldiers did not know the destination! They just followed orders.

Gen. O. O. Howard

Image 1-b

Gen. Henry Slocum

Image 1-c

Why was this done? To keep their approach from point-to-point from being ambushed by Confederate troops, of which there were not that many in the first place!

Furthermore, Sherman split the sixty-two thousand soldiers into two fingers, which would be approximately thirty-one thousand each marching randomly in some unknown direction—one slightly southeast and the other east-southeast assuming a fork-like formation. That created further confusion down the road among locals, who were wondering what in the world was going on and why were those troops doing this?

Now you would expect the thirty-one thousand soldiers to march single or double file in order to move quickly, wouldn't you? No! They marched side by side, each finger approximately twenty miles wide (some say thirty miles), a total of forty- or sixty-mile-wide swath across the face of Georgia, from which we got the scorched-earth policy and the scar across the face of Georgia. Sherman ordered General Howard and Major General Slocum to burn the fields, crops, shanties, plantations, homes, barns, livestock alive, and all the food his troops could not eat or pillage.

Furthermore, the troops took food from little children, stripped them naked, and left them out in the cold November–December weather.

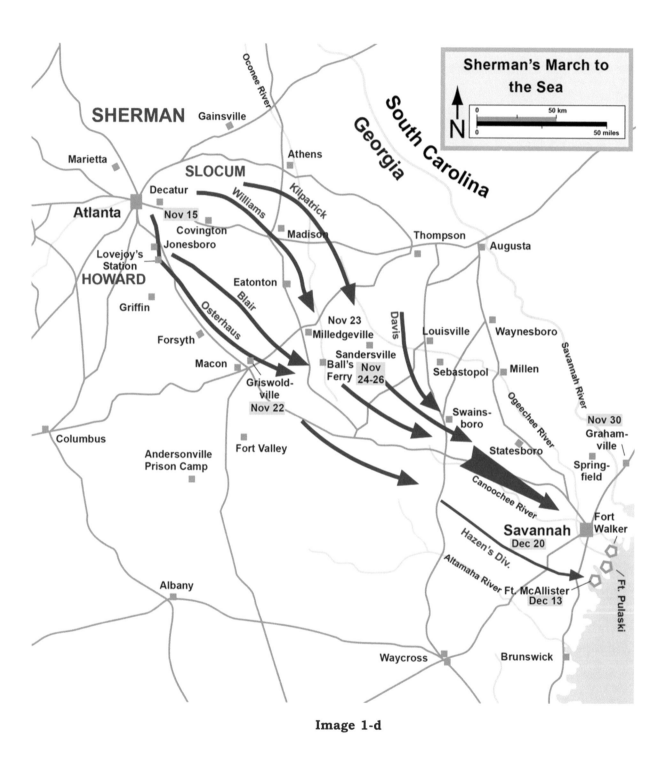

Image 1-d

Now who did that hurt? *Civilians!* Not the Confederate troops. There were very few and none nearby. These atrocities were some of the milder doses of three and a half years of war crimes designed to bring Confederates to their knees and beg for an end: in Sherman's words, "**to make**

Georgia howl." It was designed to break the Southern resolve for and devotion to the Southern Cause. As we will see later, it did not succeed.

Understanding this is critically important because most historians omit such atrocities. What caused such a violent outbreak of crimes against civilians? In chapter 1 of his book, "War Crimes Against Southern Civilians," Walter Cisco answers this concern:

> *In the midst of his 1863 invasion of the United States, Gen. Robert E. Lee issued a proclamation to his men. After suffering for two years innumerable depredations by their enemies, some Southerners, soldiers and civilians, thought at last the time had come for retaliation. Lee would have none of that. He reminded his troops that "the duties exacted of us by civilization and Christianity are not less obligatory in the country of the enemy than in our own."*

The injunction of Lee seems forgotten today but reminds us of how much has been lost in our understanding of history. Continuing on, Cisco says,

> *Through the centuries, by common consent within what used to be called Christendom, there arose a code of civilized warfare. Though other issues are covered by the term, and despite lapses, it came to be understood that war would be confined to combatants . . . which protected enemy civilians' rights as a human being during wartime.*
>
> *Yet warring against noncombatants came to be the stated policy and deliberate practice of the United States in its subjugation of the*

Confederacy. Shelling and burning of cities, systematic destruction of entire districts, mass arrests, forced expulsions, wholesale plundering of personal property, even murder all became routine. The development of Federal policy during the war is difficult to neatly categorize. Abraham Lincoln, the commander in chief with a reputation as micromanager, well knew what was going on and approved. Commanders seemed always inclined to turn a blind eye to their soldiers' proclivity for theft and violence against the defenseless. And though the attitude of Federal authorities in waging war on Southern civilians became increasingly harsh over time, there was from the beginning a widespread conviction that the crushing of secession justified the severest of measures. Malice, not charity, is the theme most often. But the kind of warfare practiced by the Federal military during 1861–65 turned America—and arguably the whole world—back to a darker age.

Th[e] principle—of people having the right to freely choose their own destiny—was utterly repugnant to Lincoln. In waging war on civilians he returned to the barbarism of the past, but he also dealt a blow to limited, constitutional government from which America has yet to recover. That all Americans are less free today, and live in a more dangerous world, are among his legacies.[2]

Now consider this: the Confederacy burn only one city, and the number burned by the Union cannot be numbered. Robert E. Lee did not sink to barbarian warfare; rather, he held on to higher principles of civil warfare.

With this 250-mile march complete in just twenty-five days, Sherman arrives about seven miles outside the city.

---

[2]   . Walter Brian Cisco, *War Crimes Aagainst Southern Civilians*, 2007, pgs. 15–20.

⤺ *Two* ⤻

Arrival outside Savannah: Hardee's Daunting Gray Stop Sign

On December 10, 1864, Sherman and his army bottleneck about seven miles west of Savannah in the vicinity of Dean Forest Road today. He and the sixty-two thousand troops immediately run into a "gray stop sign." He is stopped dead in his tracks.

The topography outside the city was different from today. Back then, Savannah sat in the middle of marshes, alligator-infested swamps, and wetlands, which provided ample acreage for rice plantations. It was impossible for wagons, cannon, horses, and soldiers to wade through the wet terrain. Beyond the seven miles going west, the topography began to rise to dry, fertile soil to support cotton plantations across the rest of the state.

Inside the city of only 22,400, Confederate general William Hardee, our hero for the moment, had ten thousand Confederate troops under his command. It was his duty to protect the civilians and the city. He positioned two thousand five hundred troops along the boardwalk of the Savannah River to prevent a potential crossing of the river by Union troops from Carolina, thereby closing the front door to Savannah. On the west, Hardee positioned the other seven thousand five hundred troops along the Central of Georgia and Atlantic and Gulf Railroad beds and the two or three dirt roads entering Savannah, closing the west-side door. The railroads and dirt roads were elevated sufficiently to allow traffic moving into the city. General Hardee did a brilliant job of designing a military strategy to protect Savannah.

General William J. Hardee

Image 2-a

Therefore, Sherman is strangled outside with no possibility of marching into the city. He immediately orders an officer to get a surrender from Savannah now. And providentially, Sherman leaves! Here begins the ten-day harrowing story of Savannah's bare survival of the Union. The map below shows the west side of Savannah when Sherman arrived.

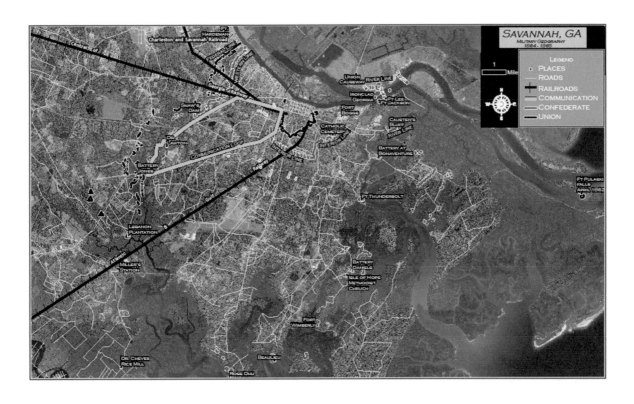

Central of Georgia Railroad, Atlantic and Gulf Railroad, and yellow dirt roads

entering the city

Image 2-b

—❦ *Three* ❦—

Capture of Fort McAllister

Having ordered an officer to get a surrender from Savannah immediately, Sherman leaves the west side door of the city with Gen. William Hazen, Gen. O. O. Howard, and four thousand soldiers heading southeast to the mouth of the Ogeechee River at the Atlantic Ocean, where Fort McAllister defended the south side of Savannah from Union naval invasions. The Ogeechee offered a backdoor route for supplies into the city. It took Sherman three days to go about nineteen miles by roads today, which would have been shorter then since troops could cut through a more direct path to Fort McAllister.

Why three full days? Considering he traveled 250 miles from Atlanta to Savannah in twenty-five days (ten miles each day), this march to Fort McAllister took three days wading through swamps and marshes to find enough solid ground to travel.

On December 13, he approaches Fort McAllister and watches, from a distant rice-mill roof two miles away, General Hazen and General Howard lead the troops into fighting position. Fort McAllister had only 230 Confederate troops defending the mouth of the river. General Hazen took out Fort McAllister in just fifteen minutes! And once again, Sherman still did not come back to Savannah, providentially! (Note the theme of this ten-day ordeal—providential grace.)

Fort McAllister 1864.

Protected by 230 Confederate troops, Gen. Hazen's 4,000 troops took out Fort McAllister in 15 minutes!

Image 3-a

⎯⚭ *Four* ⚭⎯

Sherman in Carolina with Gen. John Foster

On December 14, Sherman boarded a ship and hugged the Savannah coast, sailing north to Carolina (Hilton Head area today) to meet with Gen. John G. Foster. While Savannah is protected momentarily by General Hardee, General Foster is involved across the river with forty-two thousand Union troops in skirmishes, of which we have the upper hand for the moment. Foster is not under Sherman's command; he is Sherman's counterpart in Carolina.

Sherman's purpose to meet with Foster is to get him to place Union troops along the Savannah River on the Carolina side to prevent a possible evacuation of the city across the river into Carolina, trapping Confederate troops and civilians inside the city with the west door shut by Hardee's troops, the north door shut with Union troops, the east door shut with Fort Pulaski seized by the Union Navy in 1862, and now the south door shut at Fort McAllister. Savannah is trapped inside a sealed coffin.

However, Foster cannot and will not help. He is tied up with skirmishes in Carolina with Confederate troops who, for the moment, have the upper hand. Due to heavy Union losses, Foster, himself wounded in the leg, does not have any reserves to offer Sherman. And having no loyalty to Sherman, he will not help. He has his hands full with Confederates who are holding their own.

Gen. John G. Foster

Image 4-a

Sherman is furiously frustrated with no help from Foster and now has learned that there is no surrender from Savannah. It's been seven days since he ordered an officer to squeeze a surrender out of Savannah. Double the frustration, double the fury! Things are not going Sherman's way, providentially.

The situation in Savannah is even more desperate: sixty-two thousand troops on the west side and forty-two thousand troops across the river. Savannah is outnumbered over four and a half to one, and Hardee is outnumbered over ten to one.

—⟨ *Five* ⟩—

Hardee's Brazen Bluff

Sherman is still in Carolina now on day 7 of the ten-day standoff (December 10–20). Frustrated with Foster and learning that Savannah has not surrendered, Sherman writes a letter to General Hardee.

GENERAL:

You have doubtless observed from your station at Rosedew, that sea-going vessels now come through Ossabaw Sound and up the Ogeechee to the rear of my army, giving me abundant supplies of all kinds, and more especially heavy ordnance necessary for the reduction of Savannah. I have already received guns that can cast heavy and destructive shot as far as the heart of your city; also, I have for some days held and controlled every avenue by which the people and garrison of Savannah can be supplied; and I am therefore justified in demanding the surrender of the city of Savannah, and its dependent forts, and shall wait a reasonable time your answer, before opening with heavy ordnance. Should you entertain the proposition, I am prepared to grant liberal terms to the inhabitants and garrison; but should I be forced to resort to assault, or the slower and surer process of starvation, I shall then feel justified in resorting to the harshest measures, and shall make little effort to restrain my army—burning to avenge the national wrong which they attach to Savannah and other large cities which have been so prominent in dragging our country into civil war. I inclose (sic) you a copy of General Hood's demand for the surrender of the town of Resaca, to be used by you for what it is worth.

I have the honor to be your obedient servant,

W. T. Sherman,

Major General [3]

General Hardee receives the letter and immediately responds by daringly calling Sherman's bluff against all the odds.

---

[3]   Mills Lane, ed., "War is Hell!": William T. Sherman's Personal Narrative of His March through Georgia (Savannah, Georgia: The Beehive Press, 1974), 174-175.

General:

I have to acknowledge the receipt of a communication from you of this date, in which you demand "the surrender of Savannah and its dependent forts," on the

ground that you "have received guns that can cast heavy and destructive shot into the heart of the city," and for the further reason that you "have, for some days, held and controlled every avenue by which the people and garrison can be supplied." You add that, should you be "forced to resort to assault, or to the slower and surer process of starvation, you will then feel justified in resorting to the harshest measures, and will make little effort to restrain your army," etc., etc. The position of your forces (a half-mile beyond the outer line for the land-defense of Savannah) is, at the nearest point, at least four miles from the heart of the city. That and the interior line are both intact.

Your statement that you have, for some days, held and controlled every avenue by which the people and garrison can be supplied, is incorrect. I am in free and constant communication with my department.

Your demand for the surrender of Savannah and its dependent forts is refused.

With respect to the threats conveyed in the closing paragraphs of your letter (of what may be expected in case your demand is not complied with), I have to say that I have hitherto conducted the military operations intrusted (sic) to my direction in strict accordance with the rules of civilized warfare, and I should deeply regret the adoption of any course by you that may force me to deviate from them in future. I have the honor to be, very respectfully, your obedient servant,

W. J. Hardee,

Lieutenant General 4

However, at this moment, it appears Sherman may not have known what the tone was on this side of the river. General Hardee and his troops know it's all over (surrounded on the South, West, and North ten-to-one odds!). Mayor Richard Arnold and the city aldermen know it's all over. The civilians know it's all over. The city has run out of possibilities. If Sherman knows the tone and temperament of the city, it will be unnecessary to threaten Hardee. A surrender will come without a threat.

Whatever the case, Hardee already has plan B in place as we will see in the next chapter. [4]

---

[4]   Ibid.

—ભ **Six** ৩—

Evacuation of Confederate Troops

Having called Sherman's bluff in his letter, General Hardee had received orders from his superior, Gen. Pierre G. T. Beauregard, in Charleston, who directed Hardee to "***protect Savannah at all cost but,***"—and here comes the stinger—"***William, if you see that you cannot protect the city, evacuate the troops!***"[5]

It's hard to know exactly what that order must feel like for Hardee; his job is to protect the city. If he has to make that call, that will leave civilians vulnerable to Sherman, and God only knows what Sherman will do. Everyone knows what he did from Savannah to Atlanta. And it is hard to know what that order feels like for Beauregard too; he issued the order! But we know why the order was issued. Hardee's troops are needed across the river, where we have the upper hand in skirmishes for the moment. That means—and this is hard to grasp—the ten thousand troops are now more valuable than the civilians they are to protect at all cost!

---

[5]   . Barry Sheehy, *Savannah, Immortal City*, 2011, pg. 349.

Gen. Pierre G. T. Beauregard

Image 6-a

General Hardee already has plan B in motion. He prepared a loose, rickety, unstable pontoon bridge across the Savannah River for his troops. On the cold, wet, rainy night of December 20, all ten thousand troops got across the river by midnight. (One soldier was reported to have fallen into the cold river and drowned.) But the troops are swarmed with civilians too, trying to "get the heck out of Dodge." Once over in Carolina, they disappear into the dark, joining their comrades to engage in skirmishes.

That leaves one remaining piece of business for Savannah, as we will see in chapter 7.

Having received orders to evacuate Savannah, Hardee builds a pontoon bridge across the Savannah River.

Image 6-b

⁓ᑕᑐ Seven ᑕᑐ⁓

Mayor Arnold's Meeting and Letter

As the Confederate troops are crossing the Savannah River, Mayor Richard Arnold, on the cold, dark, rainy night of December 20, calls a meeting of the city aldermen in the old City Exchange (present day gold-domed city hall). City Exchange looks directly over the river through two windows on the north side. Two windows opposite on the south look down on Bay Street. On the west side are six windows, through which the mayor and the aldermen are able to watch the evacuation of the Confederate troops. It must have been a teary sight, full of pain and heartache, when they realize the end is near.

Mayor Arnold drafts the following letter of surrender:

> **SIR:**
>
> **The city of Savannah was last night evacuated by the Confederate military and is now entirely defenseless. As chief magistrate of the city I respectfully request your protection of the lives and private property of the citizens and of our women and children. Trusting that this appeal to your generosity and humanity may favorably influence your action, I have the honor to be your obedient servant.**
>
> **Richard D. Arnold,**
>
> **Mayor**[6]

---

[6] . Ibid., pg. 367.

Now comes the difficult part in chapter 8.

The "Long Room" of the Old City Exchange, used by the City Council for Eighty-nine years, 1815—1904.

Image 7-a

City hall today showing the six windows where Mayor Arnold and seven aldermen watched Confederate troops cross the Savannah River on the pontoon bridge on December 20, 1864

Image 7-b

——𝒞ↄ *Eight* ↄ𝒞——

Mayor Arnold and Gen. John Geary

The letter Mayor Arnold drafted now has to be received by a Union officer and accepted before there can be a surrender. The mayor secures a broken-down buggy and a nag of a mare (all the good transportation has gone across the river with civilians evacuating) and travels one mile west to a crossroad at the Old Louisville Road and the Augusta Road. The mayor brilliantly rattles his buggy to make noise and is captured by a Union soldier approximately at midnight. Once again, providentially, the soldier is not an officer and has no authority. He ushers the mayor seven miles northwest to Union headquarters at Eight-Mile Bend (US Highway 80, one mile east of I-95 today).

It is now 4:00 a.m. December 21, and the mayor is introduced to Gen. John Geary. Another providential moment! General Geary is the exact opposite of Sherman. On his March to the Sea, Sherman, with all the atrocities he committed, demonstrated his lack of civil warfare or rules of engagement for his troops with all the atrocities he committed. He gave his troops a blank check to do anything they wished to Confederate troops and civilians. But General Geary is the exact opposite. He is extremely well disciplined, has a tight leash on his troops, has them under stringent discipline, and tolerates no foolishness.

After proper introductions, Mayor Arnold gives his letter to Geary, who slowly and deliberately reads it, puts it down, and pauses. What took a couple minutes seems like hours. Mayor Arnold's heart is pounding with fear and trembling. Will it work? Will the general accept the letter and protect Savannah?

Finally, Geary utters two responses: ***"Okay. I will."*** Then he immediately turns to an officer, and like a mean bulldog, he orders, **"Stand down the troops. Do not destroy the city or hurt civilians under threat of military execution by firing squad on the spot!"**[7]

---

[7] . Ibid., pg. 368.

Mayor Arnold breathes a long sigh of relief. Now it is officially over. No more fear, no more trembling. The letter is accepted. This critical moment could easily have gone another way. General Geary could have rejected the letter, and Savannah would have gone up in flames.

What if it had been someone other than General Geary? Consider this: the mayor of Columbia, South Carolina, received the same guarantee from Sherman himself two months later, and the city went up in flames two hours later. This was another major providential moment of grace for Savannah. Oh, and Sherman is still not in Savannah yet, providentially.

Mayor Richard Arnold

Image 8-a

Gen. John Geary

Image 8-b

Approximately six to seven hours later, between 10:00 a.m. and 11:00 a.m., Sherman arrives in Savannah from Carolina. What took so long? The last we heard, he completed his letter to General Hardee and received a response on December 17, four days ago. Sherman set out to board a ship and cross over into Savannah, but providentially, his ship got grounded for three days because of an extremely low tide. But now he arrives in Savannah at midmorning of December 21, lowers Confederate flags and raises Union flags across City Exchange, and has a parade on Bay Street, celebrating the surrender of Savannah—and Sherman didn't even do it! John Geary did it when he accepted the surrender! And the civilians are seething.

Sherman checks into the beautiful Pulaski House Hotel. Built in 1835, it stood as the most beautiful, elegant, and expensive hotel in all the South. Sherman enjoyed it only one night until he had to leave. We will see why in chapter 9.

Pulaski House Hotel

Image 8-c

─♔ *Nine* ♔─

Charles Green's Brilliant Business Decision

With General Sherman in town, we approach the end of the horrific occupation of the city and visit a very prominent Savannahian, Charles Green. To understand what is about to happen, we need to get acquainted with Mr. Green. He was born in England in 1807 and grew up in Liverpool, the receiving port for cotton. During the nineteenth century, over half of England's cotton came from the South; therefore, a tight financial connection between Savannah and Liverpool—Charleston and Liverpool.

Charles Green got his feet wet in the cotton industry and, at age 26, moved to Savannah, where he and his colleague, Andrew Low, got jobs along Factors Walk. Charles and Andrew, British subjects who never changed their citizenship, formed a legal business partnership with not one, not two, but three huge gigantic incomes. First, they were not just factors; they became the big boys. They were then what Merrill Lynch and Morgan Stanley are today. Second, they owned a fleet of three ships and, on board themselves, were shipping cotton back to Liverpool. And third, on the return trip, they shipped English cargo over to America. Two shipping incomes and a factor income. These two British subjects, who never changed their citizenship, were declared two of the wealthiest men in 1850 Savannah, if not *the* wealthiest.

In the nineteenth century, the US economy bell-curved (crashed in 1892, worse than it had in 1929). In the 1850–1860 decade, the economy peaked. Charles Green married his second wife in 1850, Lucinda Ireland Hunton, from Prince William County, Virginia. His first wife, Catherine, died of tuberculosis four years earlier.

Charles's wealth peaked in 1850–1860, and before he married Lucy in 1850, Charles promised Lucy he would build her the most elegant, most ornate, most beautiful, and most expensive house in the little town of Savannah at that time (population nine thousand). Twelve thousand five hundred square feet later, three years later for construction, Charles delivered on his promise. The cost of the house must be set in the context of the average comfortable salary of twenty dollars per month for a commoner. That's $240 annually! The cost of Charles Green's house in 1850 was $93,000! And that was Charles Green and Andrew Low, and that was only a house!

Upon their marriage in 1850, Charles and Lucy took an extended honeymoon trip back to Liverpool with a shipload of cotton and, while there, went shopping and brought back then and on subsequent trips $40,000 of English furnishings, which are still in the house today—marble statues, floor-to-ceiling mirrors reflected with pure silver, white sandstone steps, and on and on. It looks today like it did in 1850.

Now this places what the $93,000 house, Charles Green, and Andrew Low represented in Savannah in the 1860s. These two gentlemen were very prominent Savannahians and very brilliant businessmen.

Back to 1864. With Sherman in town on December 21, I think this may have been the most brilliant business decision Charles Green has ever made. He extends an invitation to Sherman that while in Savannah, he will welcome the general to use that beautiful $93,000 house as his headquarters. What is going on here? Charles Green's wealth comes from the Southern Cause. Charles Green's loyalty is to the Southern Cause. And he invites the dreaded enemy from the North to use this beautiful house for his headquarters? This appears to be a disconnect!

Charles Green's House

1864

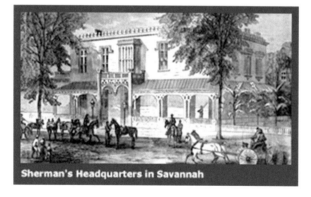

Image 9-a

TODAY

Image 9-b

That invitation does three things. First, *if* and only *if* Sherman accepts the invitation, it will preempt the norm: Union officers charging into these huge mansions, running the people out into the streets, going in to set up their headquarters, and helping themselves to a little gold and silver, if you please. For Charles Green, this is a major gamble. Will Sherman accept, or will he reject and allow his troops to rummage and pillage? Second, here's the brilliance: Charles Green knows no young, teenage blue-uniformed soldier will dare charge into the house where the general is staying and try to mess anything. But third, whose house is this really? Lucy's! Charles just wrote the check and delivered on his promise! What better way to protect *Lucy's* house than to invite the general to use it. And it works. Sherman rides down to see the house for himself and reluctantly accepts the invitation on December 22.

Sherman's reluctance is because he is not used to paying rent and wants to supply his own food, mess, and accoutrements. Charles assures him there will be no rent. His primary concern is to protect the house from possible unruliness of troops.[8]

Sherman stays in Savannah forty days with Charles Green. The entire occupation of the city, though, lasts fifty-three days, beginning on December 10, 1864, until February 1, 1865, when he and the troops leave Savannah, heading on his final leg toward Virginia and the end of the War.

Charles Green

Image 9-c

---

8   . Ibid., pg. 373.

~⌒ *Ten* ⌒~

Sherman in Savannah

Sherman's forty-three-day occupation of Savannah after arriving on December 21 was no vacation for anyone. These forty-three days were filled with important black--history moments, for which Savannah is known. One important meeting took place upstairs in Mr. Green's house when twenty prominent black ministers met with secretary of war Edwin Stanton and General Sherman to discuss emancipation, freedom, and survival for the freed slaves. This is part of black-history tours conducted in the city today. Our purpose here is just to mention the key reason for the long stay.

Upon leaving on February 1, 1865, Sherman and his troops headed north into Carolina where, when reaching Columbia, South Carolina, he met the mayor, who was prepared to surrender to Sherman, received a surrender letter, and rode off in another direction while his troops turned away and immediately burned Columbia, as mentioned earlier. That was how close we came to losing our city. It could just as easily have happened to us. Savannah was and is continually blessed with God's providential grace.

It's hard for us to imagine the horror of the military story of Savannah's survival. But Savannah was also supported by the civilian story. The Confederate Cause rang out in pulpits all across the city. Here is what Bishop Stephen Elliot of Christ Church, later founder of St. John's Episcopal on Madison Square, said:

> ***Here we are engaged in one of the bloodiest wars
> on record pressed on from every hand with the
> enemy in our very doors. There is nothing left
> to do but to follow the example of the Psalmist
> and cry unto God to give us help from trouble,***

to acknowledge that vein is the help of man. We are fighting to drive away from our sanctuaries the infidel and rationalistic principles which are seeping over the land and substituting the gospel of the stars and stripes for the gospel of Jesus Christ. Shall we for the sake of peace think for a moment, even a moment, of returning to the embrace of such a union? God forbid. Let us learn at once the stern truth that we have no country, we have no country, until we make one. We can never go back to that whence we came out. We should not recognize it in its present garb of tyranny.[9]

Civilians believed in God's presence for the Southern Cause, that God was on our side. Yet some people gave up and resigned to defeat and despair. But it was the *Savannah women* who rose to the challenge with hope.

They supported the cause fiercely. *They* loaded cartridges and became nurses. *They* made clothes and uniforms. *They* cut bandages from sheets. *They* visited and prayed for hospitalized soldiers as they took their last breath in the arms of these wonderful women. In their own way, *They* were victors.[10]

---

[9]   . Michael Jordan, Cosmo Mariner Productions, DVD, *Savannah in the Civil War,* 2012.

[10]   . Ibid.

Three cheers to the Southern Belles!

So who *really* saved Savannah? Was it General Sherman or Gen. William Hardee? Was it Abraham Lincoln or Mayor Richard Arnold? Was it Edwin Stanton or Charles Green? Was it Gen. John Geary or some insignificant other?

The great paradox is,

Savannah was saved by a Union general—John Geary!

───⌖ *Epilogue* ⌖───

In chapter 5, "Hardee's Brazen Bluff," Sherman's threat to destroy Savannah if General Hardee refused to surrender is contrasted by the fact that he never really wanted or intended to burn Savannah. This is not well known by most people. There were two reasons, military and personal. The military reason is that he needed a port city to restock and replenish his tired, hungry, spent soldiers, and he could not do that if Savannah lay in smoke and ashes. Savannah provided that need.

The personal reason he did not want to destroy Savannah is, Sherman had friends here in Savannah. One of them was the Gordon family. William Washington Gordon Sr. was born in Savannah in 1796. In 1833, he was responsible for laying the track from Macon to Savannah, 180 miles, which became the Central of Georgia Railroad. W. W. Gordon was the first Georgian to graduate from West Point Military Academy in 1815, and Sherman graduated in 1840. It is a known fact that all West Point graduates know all West Point graduates—a tight fraternity today. Gordon's son, W. W. Gordon Jr., who went by Willie, was a highly regarded Confederate soldier, although not a graduate of West Point.

But another more profound incident is, when Sherman got into the city on December 21, he sent Gen. O. O. Howard to the Gordon home to check on the Gordon's and see how they were doing. Howard visited the Gordon's and returned to Sherman with this account: "**Sir, the Gordon's are doing fine.**"

We don't know what happened to all the relationships in Savannah during and after the War. But this account of Sherman's need and desire to save Savannah was kept under his hat when he set out on his March to the Sea. As far as we know, no one knew his intentions.

Deo Vindice is the motto of the Sons of Confederate Veterans (SCV). It means "God will vindicate." That is future tense. It is our hope for preserving the Southern Cause. While future tense, there is a sense in which the first installment of vindication happened in 1865.

In April, right after Lincoln was assassinated, the federal government offered $100,000 reward for the capture of CSA president Jefferson Davis to put him on trial for treason. A conviction was certain, and execution by hanging, inevitable. He was captured in Georgia a month later in May and imprisoned. The federal government knew it could not try Davis for treason without raising the constitutional issue of secession. A Southern court would never convict Davis for treason. So the case was dropped.

Some Northern thinkers understood the moral implications. In light of all the circumstances of secession, seceded states have the right of perfect sovereignty, and the war was an invasion and conquest for which there is no warrant in the Constitution condemned by the rules of Christianity and the law of the civilized world. In a quagmire, Andrew Johnson resolved the issue with a pardon for Davis as for many other Confederates, but Davis would have nothing of it, implying guilt. He wanted a trial to clear his name.

Other lawyers confessed the trial was a loser and dropped out. After two years of imprisonment, Jefferson Davis was released. Then the chief justice of the Supreme Court came up with a solution to avoid a trial without vindicating the South. The Fourteenth Amendment provided that anyone who engaged in insurrection against the United States and, at one time, took an oath of allegiance, which Davis had done as a US senator, could not hold public office. The Bill of Rights prevented double jeopardy, and Davis, who had already been punished by the Fourteenth Amendment in not being permitted to hold public office, could not be tried again for treason. Through this episode of setting up "the trial of the century," which never happened, the South was vindicated.

On another note, as repeated many times in this story, the thread running through the fabric of Savannah's survival was God's providential grace. There is no other explanation. While the South lost the War, Savannah was one of the few cities that was spared Sherman's torch, providentially.

Finally, there are still people who nurse the notion that the War was caused by the Union's desire to free slaves. That, of course, is wrong; the War was about the constitutional right of any state to secede from the Union with no fear of reprisal. Neither the North nor the South could afford to abolish slavery. It was the centerpiece of the economy. Even if the War had been caused by the desire to abolish slavery, would that not leave the United States with a huge indelible black eye in front of the entire world? No other country fired a shot in the cause of abolishing slavery. All other nations ended slavery peacefully.

Deo vindice!

God will vindicate!

Images

*Images from the collection of Barry Sheehy and Cindy Wallace in Savannah: Immortal City

**Image obtained from NPS.

***Image from CivilWarTraveler.com

Printed in the United States
By Bookmasters